.50

D0618199

LE CORDON BLEU

HOME COLLECTION

·SOUPS·

PERIPLUS

contents

recipe ratings ❁ *easy* ❁❁ *a little more care needed* ❁❁❁ *more care needed*

French onion soup

Known in France as Soupe à l'oignon gratinée, *French onion soup has always been a very popular first course during a cold winter in Paris.*

Preparation time **20 minutes**
Total cooking time **1 hour 5 minutes**
Serves **6**

3 tablespoons unsalted butter
I small red onion, thinly sliced
3 white onions, thinly sliced
I clove garlic, finely chopped
3 tablespoons all-purpose flour
3/4 cup white wine
6 cups brown stock (see page 63) or water
bouquet garni (see page 63)
I tablespoon sherry

CROUTES
12 slices of French baguette
1 1/2 cups finely grated Gruyère cheese

1 Melt the butter in a large heavy-bottomed saucepan over medium heat. Add the onions and cook for 20 minutes, stirring often, until caramelized and dark golden-brown. This step is very important as the color of the onions at this stage will determine the color of the final soup. Stir in the garlic and the flour and cook, stirring constantly, for 1–2 minutes.

2 Add the white wine and stir the mixture until the flour has blended in smoothly. Bring to a boil slowly, stirring constantly. Whisk or briskly stir in the stock or water, add the bouquet garni, and season with salt and freshly ground black pepper. Simmer gently for about 30 minutes, then skim the surface of excess fat if necessary. Add the sherry to the soup and adjust the seasoning to taste.

3 To make the croûtes, toast the bread slices under the broiler until dry and golden on both sides.

4 Ladle the soup into warm broiler-proof bowls and float the croûtes on top of each one. Sprinkle with the grated Gruyère cheese and place under a preheated broiler until the cheese melts and becomes golden brown. Serve the soup immediately.

Chef's tip The flour can be omitted if a lighter soup texture is desired.

Cream of leek and orange soup

A delicious puréed leek and potato soup, topped with a spoonful of orange and Cointreau cream and browned under the broiler.

Preparation time **30 minutes**
Total cooking time **55 minutes**
Serves 4

✦

2 tablespoons unsalted butter
1 large leek, white part only, thinly sliced
2 potatoes, thinly sliced
4 cups chicken stock (see page 62)
2 cups whipping cream
finely grated rind of 1 orange
1 tablespoon Cointreau
fresh chervil leaves, to garnish

1 Melt the butter in a large stockpot over low heat. Add the leek with a pinch of salt and cook slowly for about 10 minutes, or until the leeks are soft.
2 Add the potatoes and cook for 3 minutes, then pour in the stock. Bring to a boil and simmer for 20 minutes. Add 1 1/4 cups of the cream and cook for another 10 minutes. Using a blender or food processor, purée the soup until smooth. Season with salt and black pepper to taste and keep warm.
3 Preheat the broiler and mix the orange rind and Cointreau in a small bowl. In a separate bowl, beat the remaining 3/4 cup cream until stiff peaks form. Fold into the grated orange and Cointreau.
4 Ladle the soup into broiler-proof bowls and top with a spoonful of the orange cream. Place under the broiler until just brown. Scatter with a few leaves of chervil and some freshly ground black pepper.

Seafood and lemon soup

Choose from a selection of local fresh or frozen shellfish to make this very elegant and refined dish.
Savor the richness of the seafood married with the tang of refreshing lemon.

*Preparation time **25 minutes***
*Total cooking time **20 minutes***
Serves 6–8

12 oz. cockles or littleneck clams
1 lb. small mussels, in shells
12 oz. cherrystone or large clams
1/3 cup dry white wine
3 shallots, finely chopped
6 fresh or frozen sea scallops
2 small squid or calamari, cleaned
1 tablespoon oil
1 1/4 cups fish stock (see page 62)
1/3 cup whipping cream
1 tablespoon chilled unsalted butter, cut up
1 small carrot, cut into julienne strips (see Chef's tip)
1 stalk celery, cut into julienne strips
1/2 leek, cut into julienne strips
6–8 small cooked shrimp, shelled
finely grated rind of 1 lemon
chopped fresh chervil or parsley, to garnish

1 Wash the cockles, mussels and clams in lots of water and repeat twice. Be especially careful with the cockles, they can be very sandy. Place the shellfish in a large pot with the wine and shallots, bring the mixture slowly to a boil and cook for 2–3 minutes, or until the shells open. Discard any shells that do not open after this time. Lift the shellfish out of the cooking liquid, remove the flesh from the shells and set aside. It may be necessary to wash any sandy cockles again.

2 Add the scallops to the cooking liquid and poach for 1–3 minutes, then remove and cut into small cubes. Cut the squid or calamari into small cubes and fry in a skillet with the hot oil, then drain on crumpled paper towels and set aside.

3 Pour the cooking liquid from the shellfish into a clean saucepan and add the fish stock and cream. Place over high heat and boil for 3–5 minutes, or until a very light sauce is obtained. Strain, then mix in the butter, shaking the pan until it has blended in.

4 Cook the carrot, celery and leek in salted boiling water for 3–4 minutes. Drain, refresh in cold water to stop the cooking, then drain again and add all the vegetables and seafood, including the shrimp, to the sauce to heat through. Mix in some of the lemon rind and check the seasoning, adding more rind to taste.

5 Serve the soup sprinkled with chervil or parsley.

Chef's tip Julienne strips are even-size strips of vegetables the size and shape of matchsticks.

Cream of cauliflower soup

In France, this soup is known as Potage à la du Barry. *It is named after a mistress of Louis XV of France, Comtesse du Barry, whose name is given to a number of dishes that contain cauliflower.*

*Preparation time **25 minutes***
*Total cooking time **35 minutes***
Serves 4

10 oz. cauliflower, chopped (¹/₂ small cauliflower)
1 tablespoon unsalted butter
1 small onion, finely chopped
1 small leek, white part only, thinly sliced
1 tablespoon all-purpose flour
3 cups milk

GARNISH
³/₄ cup small cauliflower florets
¹/₃ cup clarified butter (see page 63) or oil
4 slices bread, cut into cubes
¹/₄ cup whipping cream
chopped fresh chervil, to garnish

1 Place the cauliflower in a large saucepan with ¹/₂ cup water. If the cauliflower is not completely covered by the water, add some milk to cover. Bring to a boil, turn the heat down and simmer for 7 minutes, or until soft. Purée the cauliflower and cooking liquid together in a blender or food processor until smooth.

2 In a medium pan, melt the butter over low heat. Add the onion and leek, cover with a buttered piece of parchment paper or a lid and cook for 5 minutes, or until soft but not colored. Add the flour and cook for at least 1 minute, stirring constantly, until pale blonde in color. Remove from the heat, stir in the milk until the mixture is smooth, then return to the heat and bring to a boil, stirring constantly. Add the purée of cauliflower to the pan and season to taste. Remove from the heat, cover and keep to one side.

3 To make the garnish, bring a small saucepan of salted water to a boil and cook the cauliflower florets for about 2 minutes, then refresh in cold water. Drain well in a colander or sieve and set aside.

4 Heat a skillet with the clarified butter or oil over high heat. Add the bread cubes and fry, stirring gently, until golden brown. Remove, drain on crumpled paper towels and sprinkle with salt while warm to keep them crisp.

5 Reheat the soup, season with salt and freshly ground black pepper and pour into warmed serving bowls. Use the cream to thin the soup if the texture is too thick. Alternatively, lightly whip the cream and then stir into the soup so that the swirls show as streaks through it. Sprinkle with the cauliflower florets, chervil and croutons to serve.

Minestrone

This is a traditional version of the Italian classic. The soup can be thickened with either white beans or perhaps spaghetti, and a generous spoonful of Parmesan added at the table.

Preparation time **20 minutes + soaking overnight**
Total cooking time **1 hour 30 minutes**
Serves 6

1/4 cup dried white beans (cannellini or navy beans)
6 cups chicken stock (see page 62)
2 tablespoons unsalted butter
1 onion, sliced
2 carrots, finely chopped
2 stalks celery, sliced
2 leeks, white part only, thinly sliced
1 tablespoon tomato paste
2 slices bacon, diced
2 cloves garlic, crushed
bouquet garni (see page 63)
3 1/2 cups coarsely shredded green cabbage
1/3 cup green peas
1 cup freshly grated Parmesan

1 Place the dried beans in a bowl, cover with twice their volume of cold water, then leave to soak overnight. Drain, then rinse the soaked beans under cold running water. Heat the chicken stock in a large pan, add the drained beans and bring slowly to a boil over medium heat. Cook for 45 minutes, or until the beans are tender, skimming the surface often.

2 Melt the butter in a large saucepan over low heat. Add the onion, carrot, celery and leek and cook gently for 10 minutes, or until soft but not colored. Add the tomato paste to the pan, mix in and cook for 1–2 minutes, stirring constantly to prevent burning. Add the bacon, garlic and bouquet garni.

3 Pour the beans and their stock over the tomato mixture and stir until well combined. Season to taste with salt and pepper. Simmer the soup for 20 minutes, add the cabbage and cook until soft, then toss in the peas and cook for an additional 5 minutes. Remove the bouquet garni and season the soup to taste.

4 Ladle the soup into bowls. Serve with the grated Parmesan on the side.

Chef's tip This soup should be thick with vegetables and beans, but do make sure that it has enough liquid to still eat as a soup. Add more water, if necessary, while the soup simmers.

Cream of tomato soup

This soup is best made with fresh tomatoes that are in season and very ripe. The result is a soup with that beautifully sweet tomato flavor.

Preparation time **15 minutes**
Total cooking time **35 minutes**
Serves 6
✤

2 tablespoons olive oil
1 onion, sliced
2 cloves garlic, chopped
3 large stalks of fresh basil
1 sprig of fresh thyme
1 bay leaf
2¹/₂ tablespoons tomato paste
2 lb. very ripe tomatoes, quartered
pinch of sugar
1 cup chicken stock (see page 62)
¹/₃ cup whipping cream
fresh basil leaves, cut into thin strips, to garnish

1 Heat a large saucepan with the oil and gently cook the onion for 3 minutes, or until it is soft without being colored.

2 Add the garlic, basil stalks, thyme, bay leaf, tomato paste and the fresh tomatoes. Season with the sugar, salt and black pepper. Pour in the chicken stock and bring to a boil, reduce the heat, cover and simmer for about 15 minutes. Discard the bay leaf.

3 Purée in a blender or food processor and strain through a fine sieve. Return to the pan, stir in the cream or half-and-half and reheat gently without boiling. Check the seasoning.

4 Serve the soup in bowls or one large soup dish, garnishing the top with strips of basil.

Chef's tip If tomatoes are out of season and lack flavor, two 16-oz. cans of tomatoes can be used and will also give excellent results.

Mussel soup

This is a delicious and delicate mussel velouté soup, lightly flavored with saffron and cooked in a sauce of white wine and fish stock.

Preparation time **35 minutes + 10 minutes soaking**
Total cooking time **30 minutes**
Serves 4

2¹/₂ lb. mussels in shells
3 tablespoons unsalted butter
I stalk celery, finely chopped
4 shallots, thinly sliced
¹/₂ cup chopped fresh parsley
I ¹/₄ cups dry white wine
I ¹/₄ cups fish stock (see page 62)
I ¹/₂ cups whipping cream
2 large pinches of saffron threads
I ¹/₂ tablespoons all-purpose flour
3 tablespoons chilled unsalted butter, cut into cubes
2 egg yolks
fresh chervil leaves, to garnish

1 Scrub the mussels well. Using a blunt knife, scrape off any barnacles and trim away the hairy beard on the straight side. Discard any mussels that remain open when tapped gently on a work surface.
2 Melt 2 tablespoons of butter in a large saucepan and gently cook the celery and shallots until soft but not brown. Add the mussels, parsley and wine. Cover and simmer for 4 minutes, or until the mussels have opened. Take the musssels out of the pan and reserve the cooking liquid. Throw away any that have not opened and remove the mussels from the shells of those that have opened.
3 Strain the reserved liquid and simmer to reduce by half. Add the fish stock and 1¹/₄ cups of the cream and simmer. Add the saffron and black pepper to taste. Combine the remaining 1 tablespoon of butter and the flour together in a bowl and whisk into the soup. Simmer the soup to cook the flour and then add the chilled butter, shaking the pan until it has blended in.
4 In a bowl, mix the egg yolks and the rest of the cream together, pour in a little hot soup and then add to the pan. Do not allow it to boil, simply warm the soup or the yolks will cook to small scrambled pieces.
5 Add the mussels to the soup to heat them through. Serve garnished with some fresh chervil leaves.

Chef's tip The mussels must be alive when cooked. They deteriorate quickly and if, before cooking, they remain open, they are dead and should not be used.

Scotch broth

This warming Scottish soup is sometimes served as two courses, the unstrained broth followed by the tender meat. Traditionally made with mutton, it is now more often made with lamb.

*Preparation time **30 minutes + 1–2 hours soaking***
*Total cooking time **1 hour 30 minutes***

Serves 4

2 tablespoons medium pearl barley
12 oz. boneless lamb shoulder
2 tablespoons unsalted butter
1 small carrot, finely diced
1/2 small turnip, finely diced
1 small leek, finely diced
1/2 small onion, finely diced
1/3 cup frozen green peas
1/2 cup chopped fresh parsley, to garnish

1   Place the barley in a bowl, cover well with cold water and allow to soak for 1–2 hours. Drain the barley and rinse under cold running water. Bring a pan of water to a boil, add the barley and cook for 15 minutes, or until tender. Drain the barley and set aside.

2   Trim any excess fat from the meat, then cut the meat into small cubes. Half fill a medium saucepan with salted water and bring to a boil. Add the lamb and cook for 2 minutes, then drain and plunge the lamb into a bowl of cold water. This process will give clarity to the soup and further remove traces of fat. Rinse the pan, half fill with salted water once more and bring to a boil. Add the meat, reduce the heat and simmer for 30–40 minutes, or until the meat is tender. Strain, reserving the meat, and measure the cooking liquid to 1 quart, adding extra water if necessary.

3   Place the butter in a large saucepan and melt over medium heat. Add the diced vegetables to the pan and cook, stirring frequently, until tender but not colored. Drain the vegetables and wipe out the pan with paper towels. Replace the vegetables, then mix in the lamb, barley and peas. Add the measured stock and bring to a boil. Reduce the heat and simmer for 30 minutes, while frequently skimming the surface to remove excess fat and impurities. Season to taste with salt and freshly ground black pepper and serve the soup with a sprinkling of parsley to garnish.

Celery root and Stilton soup

Celery root tastes like a sweeter and more nutty version of celery, and is partnered here by Stilton.

Preparation time **5 minutes**
Total cooking time **40 minutes**
Serves 4

2 tablespoons oil or unsalted butter
I onion, sliced
1/2 small celery root, peeled and thinly sliced
3 oz. Stilton cheese, crumbled
fresh watercress, to garnish

1 In a large pan, heat the oil or butter and add the onion. Cover the pan and cook over low heat until the onion is translucent. Add the celery root and 1 quart water, cover and bring to a boil. Reduce the heat and simmer for 30 minutes, or until the celery root is very soft.

2 Add 2 oz. of the Stilton and purée the mixture in a blender or food processor. Return the soup to a clean pan and reheat gently. Season with salt and freshly ground black pepper to taste, bearing in mind that Stilton can be very salty.

3 Serve with the remaining cheese crumbled over the surface. Garnish with a few sprigs of watercress and some freshly ground black pepper.

Chef's tip Celery root discolors when it is peeled, so if preparing in advance, place in a bowl, cover with water and add a tablespoon of lemon juice.

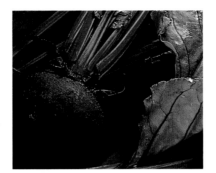

Borscht

This vegetarian Borscht is based on a recipe from the Ukraine, where Borscht is the national soup. It is characterized by its thickness and the deep red color of its main ingredient—beets.

Preparation time **40 minutes**
Total cooking time **45 minutes**
Serves 6

3 quarts water
1 tablespoon tomato paste
1 lb. fresh beets, cut into julienne strips
   (see Chef's tip)
1 carrot, cut into julienne strips
2 small parsnips, cut into julienne strips
4 stalks celery, cut into julienne strips
1 onion, finely chopped
2 cloves garlic
4¹/₂ cups coarsely shredded green cabbage
6 ripe tomatoes
¹/₂ cup finely chopped fresh parsley
¹/₂ cup all-purpose flour
¹/₂ cup sour cream
sugar, optional

1 Bring the 3 quarts of water to a boil in a large saucepan and season with salt and freshly ground black pepper. Stir the tomato paste into the liquid with the beets, carrot, parsnips and celery and simmer for about 15 minutes. Add the onion, garlic and shredded cabbage and continue to simmer the soup for an additional 15 minutes.

2 Cut a small cross in the base of each tomato and place in boiling water for 10 seconds, then immediately immerse them in cold water. Peel, quarter, seed and coarsely chop them.

3 Check the soup for seasoning and add salt and pepper to taste. Add the tomatoes, simmer for 5 minutes and stir in the chopped parsley. Thicken the soup by mixing the flour into the sour cream, then stirring it into the soup over low heat until well combined. Do not allow to boil.

4 Adjust the flavor of the soup with some salt and a little sugar if necessary. The borscht should be slightly piquant, but not sweet. The flavor is improved if the soup is made a day in advance and then reheated just before serving.

Chef's tip Julienne strips are evenly sized vegetable strips, the size and shape of matchsticks.

Shrimp bisque

The original bisque was a crayfish purée, thickened with bread. Today, all kinds of shellfish are used and the soup is usually finished with fresh cream. The result is a rich and elegant soup.

*Preparation time **35 minutes***
*Total cooking time **1 hour***
Serves 6

1 1/4 lb. small cooked shrimp, shells on

2 tablespoons unsalted butter

1 small carrot, chopped

1/2 small onion, chopped

1 stalk celery, chopped

1/2 leek, chopped

1 tablespoon brandy

1 tablespoon tomato paste

2 ripe tomatoes, cut into quarters

3 fresh tarragon sprigs

bouquet garni (see page 63)

2/3 cup white wine

1 1/2 cups fish stock (see page 62)

1 1/4 cups whipping cream

small pinch of cayenne pepper

3 tablespoons chilled unsalted butter, cut up

1 teaspoon cornstarch (optional)

fresh chopped dill weed, to garnish

1 Reserve 18 whole shrimp for decoration. Coarsely chop the remainder with the shells.

2 Heat the butter in a large pan and add the carrot, onion, celery and leek. Cover and cook over low heat until the vegetables are soft, but not colored. Add the chopped shrimp and their shells and cook gently for about 5 minutes. Add the brandy and boil, scraping the base of the pan to pick up any sticky juices, then allow the liquid to evaporate. Add the tomato paste, tomatoes and tarragon and cook for about 30 seconds, stirring constantly, then add the bouquet garni. Pour in the white wine and allow it to evaporate to a syrup before adding the fish stock and the cream. Bring to a boil, reduce the heat, cover and simmer gently for 15–18 minutes.

3 Mix vigorously and then strain through a fine sieve. Check the seasoning, adding salt and cayenne pepper as desired. Mix in the chilled butter, shaking the pan until it has blended in. The soup will thicken as the liquid takes in the butter to form an emulsion.

4 If the bisque is not thick enough, mix the cornstarch with a little cold water and then gradually whisk this mixture into the hot bisque until the desired consistency has been achieved. If it is too thick, dilute with a little more fish stock.

5 Divide the reserved whole shrimp among six bowls. Pour the soup over them and garnish with a little chopped dill weed.

Creamy garlic soup with black olive crostini

This unusual soup has its roots in the garlic-based soups of the Mediterranean. The black olive crostini would also go beautifully with many of the other cream soups in this book.

*Preparation time **20 minutes***
*Total cooking time **45 minutes***
Serves 4

1/3 cup unsalted butter
2 heads of garlic, peeled into individual cloves
2 onions, finely chopped
3 small russet or baking potatoes, cut into cubes
2 cups milk
2 cups chicken stock (see page 62) or water

BLACK OLIVE CROSTINI
4 slices of French baguette
1/2 cup pitted and finely chopped black olives
3 tablespoons olive oil

1 Melt 2 tablespoons of the butter in a medium saucepan over medium heat. Add the garlic cloves and cook for 5–7 minutes, or until golden in color. Add the onions, cook gently for 2–3 minutes, then add the potatoes and the remaining butter and continue to cook for 7–10 minutes, or until the onions begin to soften. Stir frequently as the starchy potatoes will want to stick to the pan. Pour in the milk and stock or water, then cook gently for 15 minutes, or until the potatoes are very soft.

2 Purée the soup in batches in a food processor or blender. Return to the rinsed pan and season to taste with salt and freshly ground black pepper. Cover to keep warm and set aside.

3 To make the black olive crostini, toast the four round slices of French baguette under the broiler until golden brown on both sides. Place the finely chopped olives in a small bowl and moisten with the oil to lightly bind. Season to taste with salt and freshly ground black pepper and spread onto the crostini.

4 Ladle the soup into bowls and serve with the crostini.

Thai hot and sour shrimp soup

It's worth hunting in Asian markets for the few exotic ingredients to prepare an authentic version of this unusual and delicious soup known in Thailand as Tom Yum Goong.

*Preparation time **30 minutes***
*Total cooking time **20 minutes***
Serves 4

1 lb. large raw shrimp, shells on
3 tablespoons vegetable oil
2–3 stalks fresh or dried lemon grass,
* white part only, cut into 3/4-inch pieces and bruised*
* with the side of a knife*
4 teaspoons chopped or grated fresh ginger root
3 cloves garlic
3 tablespoons coarsely chopped cilantro leaves
* and stems*
4 black peppercorns
1–2 small fresh red chiles
1–2 small fresh green chiles
4 dried kaffir lime leaves, shredded or 1 tablespoon
* grated lime rind*
2 scallions, sliced
2 tablespoons fish sauce (nam pla)
2 tablespoons lime juice
fresh cilantro leaves, to garnish

1 Peel and devein the shrimp, keeping the tails intact and reserving any heads and shells. Cover and refrigerate the shrimp. Rinse the heads and shells and dry well.

2 Heat the vegetable oil in a wide, deep skillet or wok, then add the shrimp shells and heads, lemon grass stalks and ginger root and stir-fry over high heat for 3–4 minutes. Add 6 cups water and bring to a boil, skimming the surface constantly. Reduce the heat, cover the pan and simmer for about 10 minutes. Strain the soup through a fine sieve and discard the shrimp shells, heads and seasonings. Pour the liquid into a clean saucepan and set aside.

3 With a mortar and pestle, or in a small bowl using the end of a rolling pin, mix the garlic, cilantro leaves and stems and peppercorns to a smooth paste.

4 Split down the length of the chiles, remove the seeds and cut into thin slices. You may want to wear rubber gloves as these chiles are very hot and can cause a strong burning sensation. (if you want the soup less hot, reduce the amount of chiles used.)

5 Return the stock to a boil and add the combined garlic, cilantro and peppercorns with the lime leaves or rind, scallions and shrimp. Simmer for 3–4 minutes, or until the shrimp become pink and opaque. Remove from the heat and add the red and green chiles, fish sauce and lime juice. Taste to check the seasoning. You may want to add a little more lime juice or fish sauce. Garnish with the cilantro leaves and serve.

Cream of mushroom soup

This soup combines wild and cultivated mushrooms to create a rich, complex flavor. Try using some of the new varieties becoming more widely available to create different flavors.

*Preparation time **20 minutes***
*Total cooking time **30 minutes***

Serves 6

6 oz. wild mushrooms, such as chanterelles, enoki, oyster, shiitake or cèpes
30 small button mushrooms
2 tablespoons unsalted butter
4 shallots, finely chopped
2 cups chicken stock (see page 62)
1 1/2 cups whipping cream
5–6 sprigs of fresh chervil
2 tablespoons chilled unsalted butter, cut up

1 Place the wild mushrooms in a sieve and shake off some of the sand and dirt. Thoroughly clean by tossing them in a large bowl of water, but do not leave them in the water too long as they will absorb too much liquid. Lift them out and thinly slice. Clean the button mushrooms by wiping with paper towels.

2 Melt the butter in a medium saucepan. Add the shallots and cook over low heat, covered, for 1–2 minutes. Add the mushrooms, cover and cook for 2–3 minutes. Pour the chicken stock and 1 1/4 cups whipping cream into the pan and season with salt and pepper. Add three or four chervil sprigs and simmer for 12–15 minutes.

3 Pour the soup into a blender or food processor and purée. Strain the purée into a clean saucepan, heat gently and toss in the chilled butter, shaking the pan until it has blended in. Season to taste with salt and freshly ground black pepper.

4 In a bowl, beat the remaining 1/4 cup whipping cream to soft peaks and season with a little salt and freshly ground black pepper.

5 Pour the soup into bowls. Using two soup spoons, form neat, oval, quenelle-like shapes from the whipped cream and place one on top of the soup in each bowl. Decorate with the remaining chervil.

Chef's tips If the wild mushrooms are only available as dried, use half the weight and then soak overnight in enough cold water to just cover them. The resulting soaking liquid has a strong flavor and is an excellent substitute for all or some of the chicken stock in this recipe, or can be added to stews or casseroles.

Cèpes are also known as porcini.

Smoked salmon soup with lime Chantilly cream

If at Christmas, or another special occasion, you order a smoked salmon as a whole side with skin and bones, don't throw the trimmings away. Keep them in the freezer to make this elegant soup.

Preparation time **30 minutes**
Total cooking time **1 hour**
Serves **8**

2 tablespoons unsalted butter
I onion, finely chopped
3 shallots, finely chopped
1/2 fennel bulb, finely chopped
I stalk celery, finely chopped
I leek, finely chopped
I carrot, finely chopped
1 1/2 lb. smoked salmon trimmings
1 1/2 cups white wine
bouquet garni (see page 63)
10 white peppercorns
I star anise
I tablespoon mixed fresh herbs, such as parsley
7 cups fish stock (see page 62) or water
2/3 cup heavy cream
chopped fresh chives, to garnish
2 oz. thinly sliced smoked salmon, to garnish

LIME CHANTILLY CREAM
2/3 cup whipping cream
finely grated rind of I lime

1 Melt the butter in a large saucepan over medium heat and add the onion, shallots, fennel, celery, leek and carrot and cook, stirring constantly, for 10 minutes, or until soft but not colored. Remove half the vegetables from the pan and set aside.

2 Add the salmon trimmings to the vegetables in the pan and cook gently for 2 minutes, without coloring. Add the wine, bouquet garni, peppercorns, star anise and mixed herbs and season with salt and pepper. Bring to a boil, reduce the liquid by half, then add the fish stock. Reduce the heat and simmer for 25 minutes, skimming the surface frequently, then strain through a sieve and discard the salmon trimmings, vegetables and the seasonings.

3 Transfer the liquid to a clean pan, add the reserved vegetables and cook for 10 minutes over medium heat. Strain once more, discarding the vegetables, return the soup to the pan and stir in the 2/3 cup heavy cream. Season with salt and pepper; set aside and keep warm.

4 To make the lime Chantilly cream, lightly whisk the whipping cream in a small bowl to softly hold its shape, add the grated lime rind and gently fold in.

5 Serve the soup hot or cold with the chopped chives sprinkled on top. Add a spoonful of lime Chantilly cream in the center and top with a small roll of thinly sliced salmon.

Cream of vegetable soup

You can use different vegetables for this soup depending on the season. This is a thick, winter version, but a spring vegetable soup is also delicious.

Preparation time **15 minutes**
Total cooking time **1 hour**
Serves 6

1/3 cup unsalted butter
2 potatoes, cut into cubes
I carrot, cut into cubes
1/2 onion, cut into cubes
2 small leeks, white part only, thinly sliced
I stalk celery, thinly sliced
bouquet garni (see page 63)
3/4 cup whipping cream
chopped fresh chervil or parsley, to garnish

1 Heat the butter in a saucepan, add the vegetables, cover, and cook over a low heat until soft. Add the bouquet garni. Pour on 6 cups water, bring to a boil, reduce the heat and simmer for 30 minutes. Lift out and discard the bouquet garni.
2 Purée the soup, in batches, in a blender or food processor, then strain into a clean pan and cook over low heat for 10 minutes.
3 Add the whipping cream and season to taste with salt and pepper. Serve very hot, sprinkled with the chervil or parsley and accompanied by crusty bread.

Singapore laksa

This wonderfully spicy and creamy soup, very popular in Malaysia as well as Singapore, makes an exotic and fully satisfying and substantial main course.

Preparation time **25 minutes**
Total cooking time **35 minutes**
Serves 4

❁ ❁

18 medium cooked shrimp, shells on
4 shallots, chopped
3 cloves garlic, chopped
5 dried chiles, chopped
2 stalks fresh or dried lemon grass,
 white part only, sliced (see Chef's tip)
3 teaspoons ground turmeric
4 teaspoons shrimp paste
1/2 teaspoon ground coriander
1 quart fresh coconut milk
2 1/2 tablespoons oil
2 1/2 tablespoons sugar
1 lb. skinless, boneless chicken breast halves
1 cup chicken stock (see page 62)
8 oz. dried fine Chinese egg noodles or fettuccine
whole or sliced fresh mint leaves, to garnish
1 scallion, sliced, to garnish
1 fresh red chile, seeded and thinly sliced, to garnish

1 Peel and devein the shrimp. Cover and place in the refrigerator until ready to use.

2 Process the shallots and garlic in a blender or food processor to a smooth pulp. Add the dried chiles, lemon grass, turmeric, shrimp paste, coriander and 1/4 cup of the coconut milk. Process all the ingredients to form a smooth paste.

3 Heat the oil in a medium saucepan, add the paste and fry for 1 minute, stirring constantly, until fragrant. Add 1 1/4 cups water, the remaining coconut milk, sugar and 1 teaspoon salt and stir until the mixture just boils. Lower the heat and simmer gently for 10 minutes.

4 Put the chicken in a small pan and add enough of the chicken stock to cover. Simmer for 8 minutes, covered, until cooked through, then cut into cubes.

5 Meanwhile, bring a large pan of salted water to a boil. Crush the noodles lightly with your fingers, add to the pan and simmer for 7 minutes, or until the noodles are *al dente*. Drain and rinse in warm water to remove the excess starch and prevent them from sticking together, but not to cool them completely.

6 Divide the noodles, shrimp and pieces of chicken among four bowls and pour the hot soup over. Arrange the mint leaves and slices of scallion and red chile on top and serve immediately.

Chef's tip You can replace the lemon grass with grated lemon rind to taste.

Minted green pea soup with croutons

Mint and green peas are a classic culinary partnership, here puréed together into a deliciously fragrant soup with a fairly light consistency.

*Preparation time **25 minutes***
*Total cooking time **40 minutes***
Serves 4

**1 small butterhead lettuce, such as Boston or Bibb,
  coarsely sliced**
12 scallions or 1 small onion, sliced
3 cups frozen baby peas, thawed
1–2 sprigs of fresh mint
5 cups chicken stock (see page 62)
4 slices bread
oil, for cooking
2 tablespoons unsalted butter
1/4 cup all-purpose flour
2/3 cup whipping cream

1 Put the lettuce, scallions or onion and peas into a large saucepan with the mint. Pour in the chicken stock and bring to a boil. Then reduce the heat and simmer for 25 minutes. Purée the soup in batches in a blender or food processor, then push through a fine strainer.

2 Meanwhile, remove the crusts from the bread and cut into small cubes. Heat the oil and fry the cubes until lightly browned, stirring with a spoon to color evenly. Lift out and drain on crumpled paper towels and salt lightly while hot. This will season them, but also helps to keep them crisp.

3 Melt the butter in a large saucepan over medium heat, stir in the flour and cook for 1 minute. Do not allow to brown. Remove from the heat, add the puréed soup and mix well. Return to the stove on low to medium heat and bring slowly to a boil, stirring constantly. Add the cream and season with some salt and pepper. Serve in bowls with the croutons sprinkled in first.

Chef's tip You may consider the cream optional if you wish, or lightly whisk and serve either swirled through the soup or as a spoonful on top. To vary the garnish, cook 1/4 cup extra of baby peas and use them to replace the croutons.

Fish soup

French cuisine has a number of wonderful traditional fish soups, making good use of fresh fish simmered with herbs and wine. This is a light soup, but with a surprising depth of flavor.

*Preparation time **30 minutes***
*Total cooking time **1 hour***
Serves 6

🏵 🏵

1 John Dory, porgy or sea bream, about 12 oz., filleted
4 red mullet or goat fish, about 1 1/4 lb., filleted
2 red gurnard or northern searobin, about 12 oz., filleted
1 lb. fresh eel, filleted (see Chef's tips)
3 tablespoons olive oil
1 small carrot, finely chopped
1/2 small onion, finely chopped
1/2 leek, cut into 3/4-inch cubes
3 cloves garlic, chopped
2 sprigs of thyme
1 bay leaf
1 tablespoon tomato paste
1 1/3 cups chopped fresh parsley
4 tomatoes, quartered and seeds removed
3/4 cup white wine
1/4 cup Cognac or brandy
3/4 cup whipping cream
2 large pinches of cayenne pepper
2 large pinches of saffron threads

1 Wash the fish fillets and eel thoroughly under plenty of water. Pat dry with paper towels and cut into 1 1/4–2 inch cubes. Cover and refrigerate until ready to use.

2 Heat the olive oil in a pan, add the carrot, onion, leek and garlic and cook over low heat for 5 minutes. Add the thyme sprigs, bay leaf and the tomato paste. Mix well for 5 minutes. Stir in the pieces of fish and eel and cook for another 5 minutes. Add 2 quarts water, the chopped parsley and tomatoes and simmer for about 30 minutes. Pour in the white wine and Cognac or brandy and stir over low heat for about 2 minutes.

3 Pour the mixture through a fine sieve and press very hard to take all the flavors and juices of the ingredients into the resulting liquid. Discard the fish pieces, vegetables and herbs. Pour the liquid into a clean pan and heat gently over low heat. Add the whipping cream, cayenne pepper, saffron threads and season to taste with salt and freshly ground black pepper. Cook gently for about 5 minutes. Serve sprinkled with black pepper.

Chef's tips Ask your fish merchant to scale, gut, head and fillet the fish and to skin and clean the eel.

If one kind of fish is not available, increase the amount of another fish. Eel can be replaced with a high-fat fish such as mackerel, sturgeon or herring.

Cream of asparagus soup

Asparagus is one of the most delicious of the spring vegetables. In this simple soup, which can be served hot or cold, the flavor of the asparagus comes to the fore.

*Preparation time **15 minutes***
*Total cooking time **20 minutes***
Serves 4

1 1/2–1 3/4 lb. green or white asparagus
2 cups chicken stock (see page 62)
1 cup plus 4 teaspoons whipping cream
pinch of sugar
4 teaspoons cornstarch
1–2 tablespoons water or milk
2 tablespoons chopped fresh chervil, to garnish

1 Peel and discard the tough skin from the base of the asparagus and trim the thick ends. Wash and drain. Cut off the tips 1 1/4 inches down the asparagus and set aside. Slice the stalks into thin rounds. Bring a pan of salted water to a boil, add the asparagus tips and simmer briefly for about 2 minutes. Drain and place in a bowl of iced water to stop them from cooking further.

2 Add the chicken stock and 1 cup of the whipping cream to a large pan with the sugar and some salt and pepper and bring to a boil. Add the sliced asparagus and cook gently for 10 minutes.

3 Purée in a food processor or blender, then pass through a fine sieve. Return the mixture to a clean pan and heat again. In a small bowl, mix the cornstarch with the water or milk until it forms a smooth paste. Pour a little hot asparagus mixture into the paste. Blend, return to the pan, and bring to a boil, stirring constantly. This procedure ensures a lump-free result when using a dry, starchy powder to thicken a hot liquid. Season to taste with salt and freshly ground black pepper.

4 Pour the soup into a dish or individual bowls. Swirl 1 teaspoon of cream in the center of each, arrange some asparagus tips on top and sprinkle with the chervil.

Gazpacho

This famous Spanish soup is traditionally made in a large clay bowl with ripe, bright red tomatoes.
It should be served ice cold.

*Preparation time **35 minutes + 2 hours refrigeration***
*Total cooking time **None***
Serves 6–8

I cup fresh coarse white bread crumbs
2 tablespoons red wine vinegar
2 cloves garlic
1³/4 large cucumbers, unpeeled if unwaxed, seeded
   and coarsely chopped
I onion, chopped
¹/2 green sweet bell pepper, coarsely chopped
3¹/2 lb. tomatoes, quartered and seeded
¹/2 cup olive oil

GARNISH
¹/4 large cucumber, unpeeled if unwaxed
¹/2 green sweet bell pepper
4 slices of bread, crusts removed and toasted

1 In a food processor or blender, process the bread crumbs, vinegar, garlic, cucumber, onion, green pepper, tomatoes and a teaspoon of salt in batches until puréed. Push through a strainer.

2 Return to the food processor or blender and process, adding the olive oil in a thin steady stream. Alternatively, pour the mixture into a large bowl and briskly stir or whisk in the oil.

3 Taste and season with salt and freshly ground black pepper. A little more vinegar may be required for a refreshing tang. Check the consistency, it should be thin, so you may need to dilute with a little water. Cover with a double thickness of plastic wrap and chill in the refrigerator for at least 2 hours.

4 To make the garnish, halve the remaining cucumber lengthwise and use the point of a teaspoon to scoop out the seeds. Cut the cucumber, remaining green pepper and bread into small cubes.

5 Pour the soup into well-chilled bowls and serve the cucumber, green pepper and croutons in separate dishes for everyone to sprinkle onto their own soup.

Chef's tips To serve, you could add two or three ice cubes to chill the soup, or for more color, chop a red sweet bell pepper with the green.

Make the soup a day in advance for a mature, well-rounded flavor, but cover well; the soup has a strong odor that can affect other foods in the refrigerator.

Cream of chicken soup

This soup is quick and easy to prepare. It is based on a simple stock made from chicken wings, which can be ready in just 30 minutes. You could also use the more traditional stock from the Chef's techniques.

*Preparation time **10 minutes***
*Total cooking time **50 minutes***
Serves 6

1 leek, coarsely chopped
1 small carrot, coarsely chopped
1 small onion, coarsely chopped
1 stalk celery, coarsely chopped
12 oz. chicken wings, disjointed
2 sprigs of fresh tarragon
bouquet garni (see page 63)
6 black peppercorns
1 whole clove
2 tablespoons unsalted butter
1/4 cup all-purpose flour
1 cup whipping cream
1 skinless, boneless chicken breast half
a few fresh tarragon sprigs, to garnish
2 egg yolks

1 Place the leek, carrot, onion, celery, chicken wings, tarragon, bouquet garni, peppercorns and clove in a large saucepan. Pour in 6 cups water to cover and bring to a boil, then turn down the heat and simmer for 30–35 minutes. Skim frequently for a clear finish.

2 Pour the stock through a colander and measure about 1 quart of the liquid, reserving the rest. In a medium pan, melt the butter, add the flour and cook gently, stirring constantly, for 1 minute, or until a smooth paste is formed and the flour is cooked. Remove from the heat. Pour the 1 quart of hot stock into the cooled butter and flour mixture, a little at a time, and stir well between each addition. Return the pan to the heat and continue to stir until the mixture boils and thickens. Add 3/4 cup of the cream and return to a boil. Season to taste with salt and pepper.

3 Poach the chicken breast for 8 minutes in enough of the reserved stock to just cover it. Drain and cut into small cubes. Remove the leaves from the remaining tarragon stems and place in boiling salted water, cook for 30 seconds, then drain. Mix the egg yolks with the rest of the cream and stir into the soup. Do not boil the mixture any further. Add the chicken cubes and sprinkle over some tarragon leaves and some freshly ground black pepper to garnish.

Vegetable and saffron consommé

This beautifully light consommé is very low in fat and excellent for getting you in shape.

Preparation time **30 minutes**
Total cooking time **1 hour 5 minutes**
Serves 6

CONSOMME
1 onion, coarsely chopped
1 carrot, coarsely chopped
1 stalk celery, coarsely chopped
1/2 fennel bulb, coarsely chopped
1 leek, coarsely chopped
1 cup chopped button mushrooms
2 ripe tomatoes, quartered, seeded and chopped
2 cloves garlic, halved
6 white peppercorns
small pinch of ground nutmeg
1 tablespoon finely grated orange rind
bouquet garni (see page 63)
2 large pinches of saffron threads

1 ripe tomato
1/2 small leek, cut into julienne strips (see Chef's tip)
1/2 small carrot, cut into julienne strips
1/2 stalk celery, cut into julienne strips
6 quail eggs
chopped fresh chives and chervil, to garnish

1 To make the consommé, place the vegetables into a large saucepan and add 6 cups of water. Add the garlic, peppercorns, nutmeg, orange rind, bouquet garni and a large pinch of salt. Bring to a boil, cover and reduce the heat to simmer gently for 45 minutes.
2 Strain through a fine sieve and discard the vegetables and flavorings. Measure out 1 quart of the stock, making up the volume with water if necessary, and pour into a large, clean pan. Add the saffron and set aside.
3 Cut a cross in the skin at the base of the tomato. Plunge into boiling water for 10 seconds, then put into iced water. Peel, and then with the point of a knife, remove the stem. Quarter the tomato, remove the seeds, then finely dice the flesh.
4 Add the julienned leek, carrot and celery to a pan of boiling salted water. Cook for 5 minutes, or until tender, and drain. Add these to the measured stock with the tomato and season to taste, then reheat without boiling.
5 Bring a small pan of salted water to a boil. Gently lower in the quail eggs and simmer for 3–4 minutes. Remove the shells and place each in a soup dish. Pour over the hot consommé and sprinkle with the chopped chives and chervil.

Chef's tip Julienne strips are even-size strips of vegetables the size and shape of matchsticks.

Chicken, bacon and lentil soup

Lentils are excellent for thickening winter soups and are here partnered with chicken and the traditional bacon. Brown and green lentils have the best texture for soups, but yellow and red lentils can also be used.

Preparation time **40 minutes + overnight soaking**
Total cooking time **1 hour 40 minutes**

Serves 4

1²/₃ cups brown or green lentils
I chicken, weighing 3¹/₂ lb.
3 tablespoons unsalted butter
3 oz. bacon, cut into cubes
I carrot, sliced
I small onion, sliced
I stalk celery, sliced
bouquet garni (see page 63)
2 tablespoons oil
few sprigs of fresh flat-leaf parsley, to garnish

1 Soak the lentils in cold water overnight. Rinse and drain well.

2 Remove the skin from the chicken. Then remove the breast meat and set aside. Chop up the legs, wings and the carcass. In a large stockpot, melt the butter and add the bacon and chicken legs, wings and carcass and brown over medium heat for 7–10 minutes. When nicely colored, add the vegetables, bouquet garni, 3 quarts cold water and the lentils. Place back on the heat and allow to simmer for 1 hour, occasionally skimming the foam off the top.

3 Meanwhile, season the chicken breasts with salt and pepper and pan-fry in the oil over medium heat for 5 minutes on each side, or until cooked to a golden-brown. Set aside to cool.

4 Take the chicken pieces out of the stockpot with tongs and remove the meat, discarding the bones. Place the chicken meat back in the stockpot and simmer for about 15 minutes. Remove the bouquet garni, then purée the soup in a blender or food processor. Return to a clean pan over low heat and season with salt and freshly ground black pepper to taste.

5 Cut the cooled chicken into small cubes and add to the soup to heat through. Serve garnished with parsley.

Chef's tip If you want to enrich the flavor of this soup, a few spoons of cream and butter can be mixed in just before serving.

New England clam chowder

Clams are very popular on the east coast, where they are caught in the coastal waters and eaten raw or cooked the same day. Make sure the clams you use for this chowder are very fresh.

Preparation time **40 minutes + 30 minutes soaking**
Total cooking time **1 hour 15 minutes**
Serves 4

2 lb. quahogs or large clams
1 tablespoon unsalted butter
3 tablespoons all-purpose flour
2 cups white wine
1 bay leaf
2 sprigs of fresh thyme
1 tablespoon oil
3 oz. slab bacon, rind removed and cut into cubes
1 onion, chopped
2 stalks celery, sliced
1 small potato, cut into small cubes
3/4 cup heavy cream
1 teaspoon fresh flat-leaf parsley, shredded

1 Rinse the clams under running water two or three times to remove as much grit as possible. Drain.

2 Melt the butter in a large saucepan over low heat. Add the flour and mix with a whisk or a wooden spoon and cook for 3 minutes. Set aside and allow to cool.

3 Add the wine, bay leaf and thyme to a large stockpot, bring to a boil and cook for 5 minutes over medium heat. Add the clams, cover and simmer for 5–7 minutes, or until the clams have opened. Strain, keeping the cooking liquid for later, and discard any clams that did not open. Set the remaining clams aside to cool. Once cooled, remove from their shells, chop up and set aside.

4 Strain the cooking liquid again through a fine sieve into the pan with the butter and flour mixture. Whisk together, place over medium heat and simmer for about 10 minutes, skimming the top twice, and then set aside.

5 In a large stockpot, heat the oil over medium heat and cook the bacon for 5 minutes, or until nicely colored. Reduce the heat, add the onion, cover and cook, without coloring, for 3 minutes. Add the celery and cook, covered, for 6 minutes, then add the potato and cook, covered, for 3 minutes. Pour in the thickened clam liquid, cover and simmer for 15–20 minutes, or until the potatoes are just done. Add the chopped clams and the cream and simmer for 5 minutes. Serve the soup sprinkled with the parsley.

Chef's tip Shellfish can contain lots of sand and grit. Always rinse several times, using lots of running water.

Pumpkin soup

The golden color and firm texture of pumpkins makes them perfect in soups; and the citrus fruits give a tangy taste to cut their sweet flavor.

Preparation time **30 minutes**
Total cooking time **45 minutes**
Serves 6

1¹/₂–2 lb. pumpkin (see Chef's tip)
3 large potatoes, chopped
3 large tomatoes, halved and seeded
2–3 strips orange or lemon rind
5 cups chicken stock (see page 62),
   vegetable stock or water
2 tablespoons long-grain rice
pinch of nutmeg
1 tablespoon unsalted butter, optional
¹/₄ cup heavy cream

1 Cut a wide circle around the pumpkin stem using a small, sharp, pointed knife and remove the top. Using a large metal spoon, scrape out the seeds from the pumpkin and discard, then either scrape as much flesh as possible from the pumpkin using the spoon or cut the pumpkin into wedges. Slice just inside the skin to release the flesh and chop it roughly.

2 Place the pumpkin, potatoes, tomatoes and orange or lemon rind into a large saucepan with the stock or water. Season with salt and black pepper to taste. Bring to a boil, then reduce the heat and simmer for 25–30 minutes, or until the potatoes are soft. Remove the orange or lemon rind and discard.

3 While the soup is simmering, add the rice to a pan of boiling salted water and bring to a boil. Cook for about 12 minutes, or until tender. Drain the rice in a sieve and rinse in cold water. Set aside and leave to drain well.

4 Transfer the soup to a blender or food processor and purée until smooth. Return the soup to a clean pan, add the nutmeg and adjust the seasoning. The soup should be thick, but drinkable from a spoon. If the consistency is too thick, add a little milk. Stir in the rice, butter and cream, then heat through. Pour into serving bowls and garnish with freshly ground black pepper and some herbs if desired.

Chef's tip Pumpkin is a member of the gourd family, which also includes squash. If you want, you can use other types of winter squash for this recipe such as buttercup, butternut or hubbard.

Vichyssoise

This creamy chilled leek and potato soup is an American "down home" favorite developed from the classic French version. It can also be served hot.

*Preparation time **25 minutes + 2 hours chilling***
*Total cooking time **40 minutes***
Serves 4

2 tablespoons unsalted butter
3 large leeks, white part only, thinly sliced
I stalk celery, thinly sliced
2 small potatoes, cubed
I quart chicken stock (see page 62)
3/4 cup whipping cream
I tablespoon chopped fresh chives

1 Place the butter in a large saucepan and melt over low heat. Add the leeks and celery and cover with buttered parchment paper. Cook, without allowing to color and stirring occasionally, for 15 minutes, or until soft. Add the potatoes and stock and season to taste with salt and freshly ground black pepper.

2 Bring the soup to a boil, then reduce the heat and simmer for 15 minutes, or until the potatoes become very soft. Purée the soup in batches in a food processor or blender, pour into a bowl, stir in 1/2 cup of the whipping cream and season with salt and pepper. Cover with plastic wrap and allow to cool before placing in the refrigerator to chill for at least 2 hours.

3 Serve the soup in chilled bowls. Softly whip the remaining 1/4 cup of cream and spoon onto the center of the soup. Sprinkle with chives to garnish.

Chef's tip Instead of leeks, you can use mild Bermuda or Spanish onions.

Summer shrimp and cucumber soup

An unusual and refreshing soup with its origins in the Middle East. Very easy to make, it should be served chilled, accompanied by pita bread, for a perfect alfresco lunch.

*Preparation time **20 minutes + 30 minutes standing
+ 2–3 hours refrigeration***
*Total cooking time **10 minutes***
Serves 6–8

I large cucumber
I egg, optional
I¹/2 cups chicken stock (see page 62)
²/3 cup tomato or vegetable juice
3²/3 cup Greek thick plain yogurt
¹/2 cup whipping cream
**2 oz. cooked shelled shrimp, fresh or frozen,
    coarsely chopped**
12 medium cooked shrimp, shells on
I clove garlic, crushed
I teaspoon chopped fresh mint
I teaspoon chopped fresh chives

1 Peel and cut the cucumber into ¹/2-inch cubes, salt them lightly and leave in a colander for about 30 minutes. Rinse in cold water, drain and dry on crumpled paper towels.

2 Bring a small pan of salted water to a boil, lower in the egg and simmer for 7 minutes. Lift the egg out into a bowl of iced water to stop the cooking process and tap to just crack the shell. Leave in the water until just cool enough to remove the shell, then return the egg to the cold water. When fully cooled, chop coarsely.

3 In a large bowl, mix the chicken stock, tomato juice and yogurt together. When quite smooth, add the cucumber, cream and chopped shrimp to the soup. Season to taste with salt and freshly ground black pepper. Cover and place in the refrigerator to chill for 2–3 hours.

4 Meanwhile, remove the shells from the whole shrimp, leaving any heads and tails on, then devein them. Cover and store in the refrigerator.

5 Rub the inside of the individual soup bowls with the garlic. Pour in the soup and sprinkle with the egg and chopped mint and chives. Hang two shrimp on the side of each bowl and serve immediately, accompanied by fresh bread.

Chef's tip To keep a hard-cooked egg from overcooking, it must be cooled immediately in iced water. The quick cooling also prevents an unsightly green-grey ring from forming around the yolk.

Apple and parsnip soup

Don't save your fruit for dessert—a fruit and vegetable soup makes a wonderful beginning to a meal. Granny Smiths are just right for this recipe as they are not too sweet.

*Preparation time **30 minutes***
*Total cooking time **40 minutes***
Serves 6

2 tablespoons unsalted butter
I onion, chopped
2 stalks celery, chopped
5 parsnips, chopped
3 Granny Smith or other tart cooking apples,
   peeled and chopped
bouquet garni (see page 63)
6 cups chicken stock (see page 62)
a few sprigs of fresh thyme, to garnish
chopped walnuts, to garnish

1 Heat the butter in a medium saucepan, add the onion, cover with buttered parchment paper and a lid and cook gently until the onion is transparent, but not colored. Add the celery, parsnips and apples and season with salt and pepper. Cook for a few minutes, then add the bouquet garni and cover with the chicken stock.

2 Bring to a boil, then reduce the heat and simmer for 25 minutes, or until the vegetables are soft. Skim the surface, remove the bouquet garni, transfer the soup to a food processor or blender and process until smooth. Return the soup to a clean saucepan, reseason to taste and reheat.

3 Divide the soup into individual soup bowls. Arrange a little thyme and some chopped walnuts in the center of each soup bowl to serve.

Chef's tip For a different garnish, stir 1 tablespoon of Calvados or applejack into 2/3 cup softly whipped cream. Carefully swirl the flavored cream into the soup just before serving.

Chef's techniques

◆

Making fish stock

Use white fish, rather than oily fish such as salmon, trout or mackerel. Remove the eyes and gills.

Soak 4 lb. chopped fish bones and trimmings in salted water for 10 minutes; drain. Return to a clean pan with 2¹/2 quarts water, 12 peppercorns, 2 bay leaves, a chopped celery stalk and onion and juice of 1 lemon.

Bring to a boil, then reduce the heat and simmer for 20 minutes. During simmering, skim off any scum that rises to the surface using a large spoon.

Ladle the stock in batches into a fine sieve over a bowl. Gently press the solids with the ladle to extract all the liquid and place in the refrigerator to cool. Makes 6 cups.

Making chicken stock

Good, flavorsome homemade stock can be the cornerstone of a great soup.

Cut up 1 1/2 lb. chicken bones and carcass and put in a pan with a coarsely chopped onion, carrot and celery stalk. Add 6 peppercorns, a bouquet garni and 4 quarts water.

Bring to a boil and let the stock simmer gently for 2–3 hours, skimming off any scum that rises to the surface using a large spoon. Strain the stock through a sieve into a clean bowl, then allow to cool.

Chill the stock overnight, then lift off any fat. If you can't leave overnight, skim, then drag the surface of the hot strained stock with paper towels to lift off the fat. Makes 6–8 cups.

Making brown stock

Roasting the bones gives a good color to the stock and helps to remove the excess fat.

In a 450°F oven, roast 3lb. beef or veal bones for 40 minutes, adding a quartered onion, 2 chopped carrots, 1 chopped leek and 1 chopped celery stalk halfway through.

Transfer to a clean pan. Add 4 quarts water, 2 tablespoons tomato paste, bouquet garni and 6 peppercorns. Simmer for 3–4 hours, skimming often.

Ladle the stock in batches into a fine sieve over a bowl. Gently press the solids with the ladle to extract all the liquid and place in the refrigerator to cool. Lift off any fat. Makes 6–8 cups.

Clarifying butter

Removing the water and solids from butter makes it less likely to burn. Ghee is a form of clarified butter.

To make about 1/3 cup clarified butter, cut 6 oz. butter into small cubes. Place in a small pan set into a larger pot of water over low heat. Melt the butter without stirring.

Remove the pan from the heat and allow to cool slightly. Skim the foam from the surface, being careful not to stir the butter.

Pour off the clear yellow liquid, being very careful to leave the milky sediment behind in the pan. Discard the sediment and store the clarified butter in an airtight container in the refrigerator.

Freezing stock

Stock will keep in the refrigerator for 3 days. It can be frozen in portions for later use, for 6 months.

After removing any fat, boil the stock until reduced to 2 cups. Cool and freeze until solid. Transfer to a plastic freezer bag and seal. To make 2 quarts stock, add 6 cups water to 2 cups concentrated stock.

Bouquet garni

Add the flavor and aroma of herbs to your dish with a freshly made bouquet garni.

Wrap the green part of a leek loosely around a bay leaf, a sprig of thyme, some celery leaves and a few stalks of parsley, then tie with string. Leave a long tail to the string for easy removal.

First published in the United States in 1998 by Periplus Editions (HK) Ltd., with editorial offices at
153 Milk Street, Boston, Massachusetts 02109.

Murdoch Books and Le Cordon Bleu thank the 32 masterchefs of all the Le Cordon Bleu Schools, whose knowledge and
expertise have made this book possible, especially: Chef Cliche (MOF), Chef Terrien, Chef Boucheret, Chef Duchêne (MOF),
Chef Guillut, Chef Steneck, Paris; Chef Males, Chef Walsh, Chef Hardy, London; Chef Chantefort, Chef Bertin, Chef Jambert,
Chef Honda, Tokyo; Chef Salembien, Chef Boutin, Chef Harris, Sydney; Chef Lawes, Adelaide; Chef Guiet, Chef Denis, Ottawa.
Of the many students who helped the Chefs test each recipe, a special mention to graduates David Welch and Allen Wertheim.
A very special acknowledgment to Directors Susan Eckstein, Great Britain, and Kathy Shaw, Paris, who have been responsible for
the coordination of the Le Cordon Bleu team throughout this series.

The Publisher and Le Cordon Bleu wish to thank Carole Sweetnam for her help with this series.

First published in Australia in 1998 by Murdoch Books®

Managing Editor: Kay Halsey
Series Concept, Design and Art Direction: Juliet Cohen
Food Director: Jody Vassallo
Food Editors: Lulu Grimes, Kathy Knudsen, Tracy Rutherford
Designer: Annette Fitzgerald
Photographer: Joe Filshie
Food Stylist: Carolyn Fienberg
Food Preparation: Jo Forrest
Chef's Techniques Photographer: Reg Morrison
Home Economists: Michelle Lawton, Kerrie Mullins, Kerrie Ray

Library of Congress catalog card number: 98-65440
ISBN 962-593-434-0

Front cover: New England clam chowder

Distributed in the United States by
Tuttle Publishing
Distribution Center, Airport Industrial Park, 364 Innovation Drive
North Clarendon VT, 05759-9436
Tel: (802) 773-8930
Fax: (802) 773-6993

Printed in Singapore

05 04 03   10 9 8 7 6 5 4 3

Important: Some of the recipes in this book may include raw eggs, which can cause salmonella poisoning.
Those who might be at risk from this (the elderly, pregnant women, young children and those suffering
from immune deficiency diseases) should check with their physicians before eating raw eggs.